Our Restless Earth

COASTS
AND ISLANDS

Terry Jennings

Silver Burdett Press
Parsippany, New Jersey

First published in Great Britain in 1998 by

Belitha Press Limited,
London House, Great Eastern Wharf,
Parkgate Road, London SW11 4NQ

Editor: Julie Hill
Designers: Steve Wilson, Maria D'Orsi
Illustrator: Graham Rosewarne
Picture researcher: Diana Morris
Consultant: Stephen Watts

Published in the United States in 1998 by
Silver Burdett Press
A Division of Simon & Schuster
299 Jefferson Road
Parsippany, New Jersey 07054-0480

Library of Congress Cataloging-in-Publication Data
Jennings, Terry.
Coasts and islands/by Terry Jennings.
p.   cm.—(Our restless earth)
Includes index.
Summary: Discusses how oceans shape coastlines, how islands are formed, how people
use coasts, and how people may damage them.
1. Coasts—Juvenile literature. 2. Islands—Juvenile literature. [1. Mountains. 2. Islands.]
I. Title. II. Series: Jennings, Terry J. Our restless earth.
GB451.2.J46   1998   97-36098
551.45'7—dc21   CIP   AC

(LSB) ISBN 0-382-39945-5   10   9   8   7   6   5   4   3   2   1
(PBK) ISBN 0-382-39946-3   10   9   8   7   6   5   4   3   2   1

Printed in Hong Kong

Photographic credits

Bruce Coleman Ltd: front cover & 8 Harald Lange, 4, 5t Hans-Peter
Merten, 19b Dieter & Mary Plage. **James Davis Travel Photography:**
13b. **Eye Ubiquitous:** 13t Sylvia Greenland. **FLPA:** 7t & 7b Maurice
Nimmo, 25b M. B. Withers, 26 W. Broadhurst. **Getty Images:** 29b. **GSF:**
19t. **Terry Jennings:** 10, 16, 23. **Still Pictures:** 27 & 28 Mark Edwards.
Woodfall Wild Images: 11 David Woodfall, 15 M. Barlow, 20 Lawson
Wood, 25t & 29t David Woodfall. **Zefa:** back cover & 5b Bell, 14 Deckart,
title page & 17 Schmied, 21 Schafer, 22 Weir.

Words in **bold** appear in the Glossary on pages 30 and 31.

Contents

Powerful seas

The sea is a powerful force of nature that constantly changes the shape of our planet. It wears away the land and helps to form new land.

Changing coastlines

A coast is the place where land meets the sea. All the time the coast is being changed by the sea. The seashore lies along the coast, and there are sandy, muddy, and rocky shores. Some seashores have **cliffs** behind them.

▲ Many people go to the coast for their vacations. Coastal towns, like this one in northern Spain, often have high-rise hotels and crowded beaches.

New land for old

In some places the sea destroys the land. In other places new land grows out into the sea. New land is formed from the tiny pieces of rock the sea has carried from other places.

The sea can also make **islands**. These are pieces of land the sea has cut off from the **mainland**.

Some islands in warm, clear waters are made by sea animals called **corals**. Other islands are made by volcanoes under the sea.

Using the coast

Many people go to the coast for their vacations or to enjoy sports and hobbies. Some of our food comes from the coast. Salt, oil, and gas also come from coastal areas. Sheltered parts of the coast are used as ports for ships and fishing boats.

Coasts and islands

In this book we look at how the sea changes the land and how islands are formed. We also look at how we use coasts and how we are in danger of damaging them.

▲ The port of Oslo in Norway. Boats and ships sail all over the world from this port.

◄ This island is part of the Togian Islands in Indonesia. It is a coral island, formed by tiny sea animals.

Moving sea water

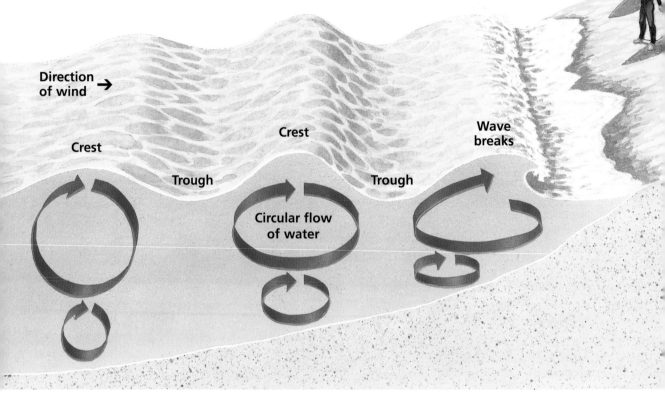

Direction of wind →

Crest

Crest

Wave breaks

Trough

Trough

Circular flow of water

▲ *Waves are formed by wind blowing over the oceans. The water in each wave stays almost in the same place, going around and around.*

The water in the oceans and seas is always moving because of **waves, currents**, and **tides**. This moving water wears away the land on the coast. It also carries away small pieces of rock.

Waves at work

Waves are made by the wind blowing across the water. In the open sea, waves look as if they are moving forward, but really the water in a wave moves in a circle. Near the shore some of the moving water rubs against the seabed. This slows the wave down so that its top curves over, or **breaks**.

High tide, low tide

The level of the sea rises twice a day in most parts of the world and covers the shore. Twice a day the level of the sea falls, and the tide goes out.

The sun and moon pull on the seas nearest to them, making them bulge up. There is another bulge on the opposite side of the earth. As the earth spins each day, so places by the sea move into these bulges, and their sea levels rise and fall.

▲ *At low tide the sea level falls, and the harbor empties.*

Flowing currents

Currents are like giant rivers flowing across the oceans. Warm currents, created by winds, flow near the surface of the water. Cold currents are caused when cold water near the polar regions sinks, making a current deep down in the ocean.

▲ *At high tide the sea level rises, and water fills the harbor.*

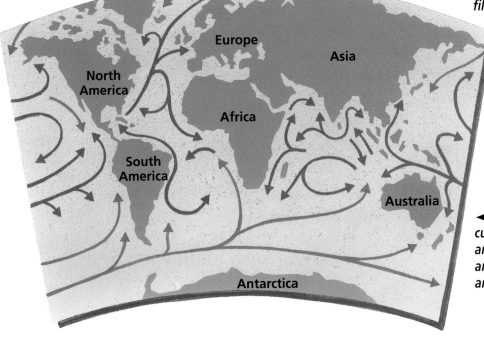

◄ *The world's ocean currents. Cold currents are shown in blue and warm currents are shown in red.*

Changing rock faces

▲ *The sea has carved this coastline in Australia into headlands, bays, and stacks.*

Where high ground meets the sea, there are steep rock faces called cliffs. Cliffs are constantly attacked by the sea. They move slowly inland as the sea wears away, or **erodes**, their rock.

Wearing away

Cliffs erode fastest at their bases. Waves throw rocks and pebbles at the foot of a cliff, slowly wearing away its bottom until the rocks above collapse. The erosion of the cliff base continues so that the cliff crumbles farther and farther back. A flat area of rock, called a **wave-cut platform**, is left at the bottom of the cliff.

The sea erodes cliffs in two other ways. As waves hit the cliff, the water forces air into cracks between the rocks, breaking them up. Sea water also **dissolves** some rocks, such as chalk and limestone.

Bays and headlands

When a cliff is made of hard and soft rocks, the soft rocks wear away first. The soft rocks are worn away to make **bays**, while the hard rocks are left jutting out as **headlands**.

Arches, stacks, and caves

The waves may slowly cut a hollow into a cliff, forming a **cave**. They may then punch a hole, called a **blowhole**, through the roof of the cave. Caves on opposite sides of the headland may meet to form an **arch**. If the roof of the arch falls in, it leaves a column of rock called a **stack**. In time the stack will be worn away completely.

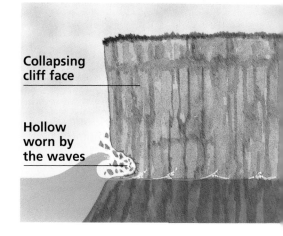

Collapsing cliff face

Hollow worn by the waves

Cliff used to come to here

Wave-cut platform

▼ *How the hard and soft rocks of the coastline are eroded and changed by the power of the sea.*

▲ *How a cliff is worn away to form a wave-cut platform.*

Blowhole

Bay made of soft rock

Stack formed when the top of an arch collapses

Headland made of harder rock

Arch where two caves meet

Cave where waves have cut a hollow in a weak area of cliff

Building beaches

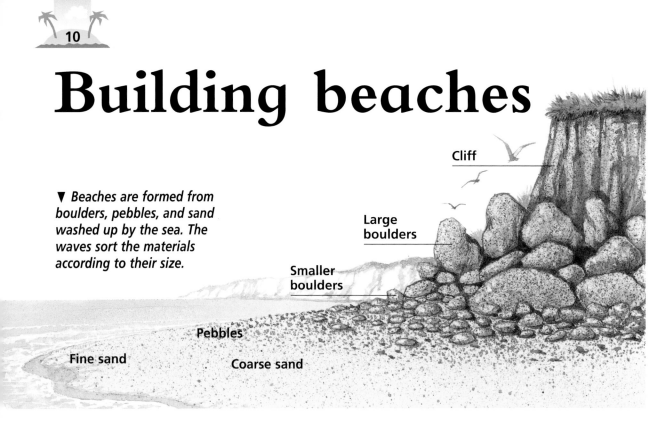

▼ Beaches are formed from boulders, pebbles, and sand washed up by the sea. The waves sort the materials according to their size.

Cliff

Large boulders

Smaller boulders

Pebbles

Coarse sand

Fine sand

▼ Storms have carried large boulders to the back of this sandy beach. This type of beach is called a storm beach.

Beaches are strips of land at the sea's edge. In open, windy places a beach is usually made of **pebbles**. Where the coast is sheltered, a beach is often made of **sand**.

Boulders to pebbles

When the waves wear away cliffs, large pieces of rock break off and crash down onto the beach. There they are broken down by the waves into smaller pieces. The large pieces of rock are called **boulders**. These are pounded into smaller pieces, called pebbles. The pebbles are swept along by tides and currents, wearing them away until they become sand.

Forming beaches

Rivers bring millions of tons of sand and mud to the oceans every year. More sand is produced when cliffs are worn away by the sea. Beaches are made from sand and pebbles washed up by the sea. Bigger pebbles are pushed up to the back of the beach at high tide. Smaller pebbles and sand are washed down the slope by the outward flow, or **backwash**.

Stormy beaches

At the back of some beaches, there are very large boulders that were carried there during storms. These are called storm beaches.

▲ Marram grass is able to grow on the loose sand of a sand dune. Eventually the sand dune may form new land.

Hills of sand

If the wind blows toward a sandy shore for most of the year, it may pile up the sand to form hills called **sand dunes**. Sometimes dunes move inland and bury houses, churches, and forests.

Some of the most spectacular dunes in the world are the Pillat Dunes near Arcachon in France, Las Marismas in Spain, the Raabjerg Mile Dune in Denmark, and the dunes on Bodie Island on the Atlantic Coast of the United States.

Drifting sands

Waves move sand and pebbles along the shore. These materials may help to form new land farther along the coast. But moving sand and pebbles can also destroy beaches and block harbors.

Longshore drift

Waves move sand and pebbles by **longshore drift**. This happens in places where the wind blows the waves toward the shore at an angle. Instead of going back the way it came, the water flows back down the beach, making a zigzag pattern. Any sand and pebbles carried by the waves slowly travel along the shore in the same zigzag pattern.

▼ *How longshore drift moves sand and pebbles along the shore in a zigzag pattern.*

Disappearing beaches

Longshore drift can cause problems. Harbors can be blocked by sand dumped by the ocean. Whole beaches can be carried away, often in the space of a year. Some vacation resorts have to bring in sand to fill the beach.

Direction of moving sand and pebbles

Waves move toward the shore at an angle

Waves are slowed down by **groynes** on the beach.

The waves drop the sand they were carrying and the beach gets wider.

New land

Where the wind blows in the same direction most of the time, sand and pebbles can be carried over great distances by longshore drift. The sand and pebbles are carried along until the angle of the shore changes —often at a bay or the mouth of a river, where the ocean is deeper. This makes the waves move slowly so that they drop the materials they were carrying. New land is then formed.

▲ *A dredger is used to pump sand back to this beach on the Spanish island of Ibiza. Dredgers replace the sand washed away by longshore drift.*

Spits and bars

In time the sand and pebbles may pile so high that they form a ridge across the bay or river mouth. This ridge is called a **spit**. If the spit grows all the way across the **inlet**, it is called a **bar**. The shallow pool of water left behind the bar is called a **lagoon**. If a spit builds up across the mouth of a river, it may force the river to find a new outlet to the ocean.

◄ *A bar has been formed by piles of sand and pebbles across this bay. A lagoon can be seen behind the bar.*

Defending the land

▲ *These groynes on this stormy coastline slow down moving water and stop the waves from wearing away the land.*

Along some coasts the sea quickly wears away the land. Farmland, houses, and beaches may be destroyed. In some places people spend huge sums of money on sea defenses. These are ways of trying to hold back the sea so that it does not damage the land and the beaches along the shore.

Walls of concrete

Sometimes a sea wall is built. This is like a cliff, but it is made from concrete. Most modern sea walls are curved so that they push the waves up, around, and back out to sea again. This stops the waves from damaging the coast.

Beach fences

Groynes are fences built on beaches at right angles to the sea. They slow down the water currents and stop sand and pebbles from being washed away from the beach by longshore drift. But over the years groynes rot away or are worn away by the force of the sea and have to be replaced.

◄ *A sea wall makes waves curve back and go out to sea again so that they do not erode the coast.*

Tetrapods

Waves break

◄ *These breakwaters are called tetrapods. They break up the force of the waves before they reach the shore.*

Breaking the waves

Breakwaters are long barriers of large boulders or concrete shapes built out into the sea. These break up the force of the waves before they reach the shore. They also protect boats and ships in harbors from damage during stormy weather.

Dune damage

Sand dunes are easily damaged by people walking over them. When the wind blows strongly, the dunes may be blown away, allowing the sea to flood inland. To prevent this, people plant grasses, such as marram grass, to help hold the dunes in place. Trees are also planted on them to stop them from moving inland and burying roads and buildings.

► *Breakwaters in this harbor in Chile, South America, help to protect boats and ships during stormy weather.*

Islands

Islands are pieces of land surrounded by water. There are thousands of islands in the oceans and seas of the world. Some islands, such as Greenland and Madagascar, are huge masses of land. Other islands are tiny. There are two main kinds of island: **oceanic islands** and **continental islands**. These were formed in different ways.

Continental islands

Continental islands are close to the mainland. Thousands of years ago many of them were joined to the mainland. They became islands because the sea level changed, cutting off pieces of land. Continental islands include the British Isles, Japan, Hong Kong, Trinidad in the Caribbean Sea, and Madagascar in the Indian Ocean.

▲ *A small continental island being formed off the coast of Minorca, Spain.*

Rising sea levels

Continental islands may form because the land sinks or because the sea level rises. Where this happens, only the high ground is left above water, forming islands. For example, the British Isles were once part of mainland Europe.

After the **Ice Age** huge areas of ice and snow melted, and the extra water made the sea level rise. Water swept over the dry land that we now call the North Sea and the English Channel. The British Isles were left standing in the sea.

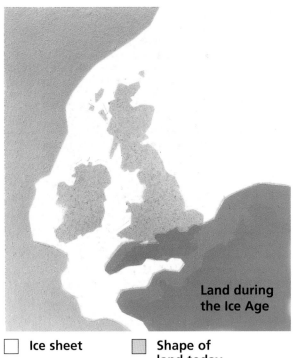

Land during the Ice Age

□ Ice sheet   □ Shape of land today
■ Land

▲ *During the Ice Age the British Isles were connected to the rest of Europe (left). When the ice sheets melted, they became separate continental islands as they are today (right).*

North Sea

English Channel

Sinking land

In some places dry land sank into the sea. Only the tops of mountains were left standing above the water. This formed a group of islands called an **archipelago**. The archipelagos off the west coast of Scotland and to the west of Canada were formed in this way. Continental islands are very much like the mainland from which they have been separated.

▶ *The Maldives are an archipelago in the Indian Ocean. They were formed where dry land sank, leaving the high ground above sea level.*

Oceanic islands

A volcano erupts on the sea bed.

Further eruptions cause the volcano to grow.

The volcano appears above sea level as an island.

▲ *The formation of a volcanic island. Each eruption builds up more land until it appears above sea level.*

Oceanic islands lie far out to sea, away from any other land. Many oceanic islands were made by undersea volcanoes. In warmer seas, oceanic islands were often made by tiny coral animals. There are hundreds of oceanic islands in the Pacific Ocean, including the Hawaiian Islands and the Galapagos Islands. Ascension Island, St. Helena, and Iceland are oceanic islands in the Atlantic Ocean.

Undersea volcanoes

The earth's crust is made up of 20 or more pieces, called plates. These plates are always moving—slowly pushing together, pulling apart, or sliding past each other. Most volcanoes, both on land and under the sea, are where two or more plates meet.

Volcanic islands

Many oceanic islands are the tops of high mountains. These mountains were formed when a volcano on the seabed erupted. The molten rock, or lava, together with the ashes that came out of the volcano, slowly built up a mountain beneath the sea. Iceland is an example of a volcanic island. It grows each time the volcanoes on it erupt. Other examples of volcanic islands include White Island off the coast of New Zealand, Stromboli off the coast of Italy, and Surtsey off the coast of Iceland.

Islands disappear

Sometimes volcanic islands disappear. This is what happened to the island of Anak Krakatoa between Java and Sumatra in the Indian Ocean. It first appeared in 1927. Since then it has disappeared beneath the surface of the ocean and then reappeared. The last time it appeared above the ocean was in 1950, and it is still there. Perhaps one day it will disappear again.

▲ *A volcanic eruption on the seabed off the coast of Iceland in 1963 produced a new island. This island is called Surtsey.*

▶ *Anak Krakatoa or "child of Krakatoa" first appeared in the crater of Krakatoa in 1927. It now forms a separate volcano.*

Islands of coral

▲ *These corals in the Red Sea provide a home for many species of fish and other sea animals and plants.*

Corals are small, brightly colored sea animals. They have tiny tentacles for catching food. Most corals live in places where the seas are warm, clean, and shallow.

Old corals, new corals

Each coral makes a cup of limestone around its soft body for protection. When the animal dies, its cup is left behind. New corals grow on top of old ones. They often form beautiful shapes like branches or fans.

Coral reefs

Very slowly a tall wall of coral builds up from the bottom of the sea. It is called a **coral reef**. Many fish shelter in coral reefs and in the seaweeds that grow on them.

Reefs and islands

Reefs grow upward from the seabed until they are just beneath the surface of the sea. Ships are sometimes wrecked on coral reefs.

Some reefs grow close to the shore. These are called **fringing reefs**. Some fringing reefs form on the tops of underwater volcanoes. If the sea level falls, or the volcano wears away, the top of the reef is left standing above the water. The reef is now a **barrier reef**. As the volcanic island continues to sink, a circle of coral islands is formed, called an **atoll**. The pool of sea water left in the middle of the atoll is called a lagoon.

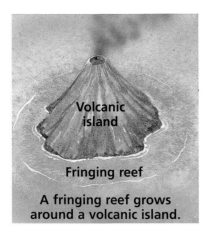

Volcanic
island

Fringing reef

A fringing reef grows
around a volcanic island.

The island begins to sink and
the reef is now a barrier reef.

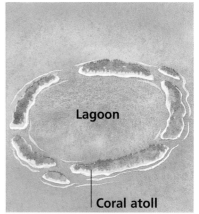

Lagoon

Coral atoll

Reefs and wildlife

The water flowing over a coral reef carries
a great deal of food. This, and the shelter
the reef provides, means the area around
the reef is full of sea animals. Nowhere
else in the ocean are there so many different
animals. In one part of the Great Barrier
Reef off the coast of Australia, there are
about 2,000 different species.

▲ *A coral island atoll begins
life as a fringing reef around
an underwater mountain or
volcano. The volcano wears
away until only the top of the
reef stands above the water.*

▼ *The Blue Hole, in Belize in
the Caribbean Sea, is a coral
island atoll.*

Up and down

The level of the oceans has not always stayed the same. In some parts of the world, the sea level has risen. In other places, land has been forced upward, pushing beaches and cliffs above sea level.

Drowned coastlines

Over the last 18,000 years, the sea level has risen about 400 feet. This happened because, at the end of the Ice Age, the ice and snow that covered much of the land began to melt. Many low-lying coastal areas were flooded as sea water rushed inland. The result is drowned coastlines. In some places at low tide, it is possible to see the remains of forests that were flooded and killed when the sea level rose.

Fiords, lochs, and rias

The **fiords** of Norway and the sea lochs of Scotland were formed during the Ice Age. At that time these inlets were filled with slow-moving glaciers, which flowed from far inland. The glaciers carved out deep, steep-sided valleys. When the ice melted, the sea level rose.

▲ *This is the Sogne Fiord in Norway. It was formed by glaciers during the Ice Age.*

The valleys were then flooded. Many river valleys were also drowned, forming **rias**. These are not as deep as fiords and their sides are less steep.

Disappearing cities

Some scientists believe that the ice and snow around the North and South Poles will continue to melt. This is because air pollution may be making the world's climate warmer. A few scientists believe that if this continues, the sea level may rise another 100 feet, and low-lying cities such as New York, London, and Rio de Janeiro will disappear.

Rising coastlines

In some places movements of the earth's surface have forced the land upward. This has pushed beaches and cliffs above sea level. These beaches are called **raised beaches**.

▲ *The flat edge near the ocean is a raised beach. Once it was at sea level, but now it is several feet above the highest storm waves. The steeper ground is the old cliff line.*

▼ *A raised beach is formed when movements of the earth's crust push beaches and cliffs above sea level.*

Old cliffs

Cave

Raised beach

New cliffs

New shoreline

Plants and wildlife

The deep, open waters of the sea change little from day to day. The seashore, on the other hand, changes a great deal as the tide rises and falls. It is sometimes wet, sometimes dry. Gales and strong winds build huge waves that crash against the coastline.

Living on the seashore

Every animal and plant of the seashore is adapted to living in these difficult conditions. Many are able to live both in and out of water. Some plants and animals can survive for long periods of time out of water.

Rock pools

Many animals and plants are found in rock pools where they are sheltered from the waves. Limpets and barnacles cling to the rocks. They feed when the tide is in. Fish, such as blennies and pipe fish, live among the seaweeds, while starfish and crabs shelter under rocks.

▼ A section through a rock pool. Rock pools contain a variety of plant and animal life.

Seaweed

Limpet

Barnacle

Sea anemone

Pipe fish

Hermit crab

Blenny

Crab

Starfish

◄ *Many small animals live in the mud of an estuary. They provide food for large flocks of birds, such as these Brent geese.*

▼ *Gannets nest in large colonies on cliffs. They fly out to sea to catch fish.*

Wet sand creatures

A few animals, such as razor clams, cockles, lugworms, and the burrowing starfish, can live in wet sand. A **shingle beach**, with its constantly moving pebbles, is too dangerous for animals, although some plants can grow there. Millions of small animals live in the mud of **estuaries**. These animals live through the regular changes from salty sea water to fresh river water. They also provide food for fish at high tide and food for ducks, geese, and wading birds at low tide.

Cliff wildlife

Some plants can grow on the rocky faces of cliffs. These plants are flat and so are not harmed by the strong salt winds. Many sea birds nest and rest on cliffs, safe from their enemies.

Using the coast

▲ *This is a salmon fish farm in Hyen Fiord in Norway.*

Coasts provide us with both food and electricity. Some sheltered parts of coasts are used as ports. Salt and fuels such as oil and gas come from some coastal waters.

Catching fish

Fish and shellfish are found in great numbers in the shallow waters near coasts. From nearby fishing ports, boats catch fish using nets. Special traps are lowered to the bottom of the ocean to catch shellfish such as crabs and lobsters.

Farming fish

Fishing from boats can be dangerous in bad weather. In some sheltered bays and estuaries, fish and shellfish are farmed, or bred in special places. This is done with shellfish such as crabs, lobsters, oysters, mussels, and prawns. Certain fish, such as salmon, plaice, and sole, are also farmed.

Fuel from the sea

Much of the world's oil and gas is pumped from the rocks of the seabed. Oil and gas are easiest to obtain from the shallow waters near a coast. In deeper waters a drilling platform, or rig, is used to drill a well down to the fuels.

Power plants

On the north coast of Brittany in France is the world's first power plant to use the energy of the tides to produce electricity. Along the coasts of many other countries, there are power plants that use coal, oil, gas, or nuclear fuels to produce electricity. These power plants take in sea water to make the steam that turns the generators to produce electricity.

▲ *A salt pan in Sri Lanka in the Indian Ocean. The climate in Sri Lanka is warm enough for sea water to evaporate in the sun to produce salt.*

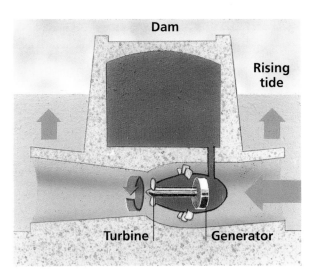

Minerals from the sea

Sea water contains valuable minerals. Salt is one of the most important of these minerals. In countries with a warm climate, water is pumped into large, open-air ponds, called salt pans. The sea water is allowed to dry up, or evaporate, in the sun. The salt is then left behind.

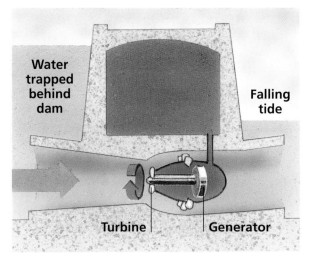

◄ *A tidal power plant uses the energy of the rising and falling tides to turn the generators that produce electricity.*

Cleaner coasts

Our coasts are very important for tourism. Many people also use the coast for swimming, boating, fishing, and water skiing. Unfortunately many coasts are polluted by litter, **sewage**, oil, and chemicals.

Harmful litter

Some people drop litter when they visit the coast. More litter is washed up from ships at sea. This litter not only destroys the beauty of the coast, it can also be dangerous. It is easy to step on broken glass left on the beach. Certain types of plastic litter can also kill birds, seals, and other wildlife.

Sewage dumping

Human waste from towns and cities is carried away in drains.

▼ *A crowded beach in the vacation resort of Rimini in Italy. Beaches like this quickly become dirty with litter.*

In some places this sewage is pumped straight into the ocean. It is later washed up on the shore. The sewage may spread germs, and it can also poison shellfish that are later eaten by people.

Poisonous chemicals

Wastes from factories and power plants and chemicals used on farms are often washed into rivers. Rivers carry the wastes and chemicals down to the ocean, where they may poison sea birds and fish.

Oil pollution

Oil spilled from ships and rigs, or deliberately dumped, can pollute the ocean. Oil kills sea birds and fish. It also washes up on beaches, making them unfit for people to use.

Caring for our coasts

Many countries now have strict laws to make sure that waste chemicals and sewage are made safe before being put into the ocean. There are also laws to prevent people from dropping litter and ships from dumping waste oil. Where these laws are in place, the water and beaches are cleaner.

▲ *These rock pools are covered in oil after spillage from an oil tanker. Every living thing in the rock pool will die.*

▶ *A beautiful, unspoiled beach in the Seychelles Islands in the Indian Ocean.*

Glossary

arch A curved opening in a sea cliff.

archipelago A group of islands formed when land sinks into the sea, leaving only the tops of mountains above sea level.

atoll A horseshoe-shaped or circular reef of coral around a lagoon.

backwash The water from a broken wave that flows back down the beach toward the ocean.

bar A ridge of sand or pebbles across a bay or river mouth.

barrier reef A long coral reef separated from the coast by a deep lagoon.

bay Where the shore curves inward.

blowhole A hole in cliffs near the ocean. Air and water are forced out of the blowhole by the force of crashing waves.

boulder A large piece of rock.

break When a wave topples over onto the shore, we say that it breaks.

breakwater A wall built out into the sea to protect the coast from heavy waves.

cave A hollow, underground place.

cliff A steep rock face, especially on the coast.

continental island An island that lies close to the mainland.

coral The skeletons of tiny sea animals.

coral reef An underwater ridge formed by tiny coral animals.

current The movement of ocean water in a particular direction. There are warm and cold ocean currents.

dissolve To make a solid substance or gas break up and change into a liquid.

erode To wear away land. Land is eroded by wind, moving water, or ice. It is then carried away and dropped in other places, especially in the ocean.

estuary The wide mouth of a river where fresh water meets sea water.

fiord An inlet of the sea between high cliffs.

fringing reef A coral reef that grows near the shore.

groyne   A beach fence built at right angles to the ocean, to stop sand from being washed away.

headland   A piece of land sticking out into the ocean.

Ice Age   A time of extreme cold that began about a million years ago and ended about 10,000 years ago.

inlet   A narrow opening in a coastline.

island   A piece of land with water all around it.

lagoon   Sea water enclosed by a coral reef. Also a shallow lake separated from the sea by a sandbank or spit.

longshore drift   The slow shifting of sand and pebbles along a beach when waves move toward the shore at an angle.

mainland   The main part of a country, not the islands around it.

oceanic island   An island that lies far out to sea, away from the continents.

pebble   A small, rounded stone.

raised beach   A beach that has been lifted well above sea level because the land surface has been raised.

ria   A narrow inlet of the sea, formed where part of a river valley has become covered in sea water.

sand   Tiny grains of worn-down rock.

sand dunes   Hills formed by wind-blown sand.

sewage   The waste material and liquid from houses and factories, carried away by drains or sewers.

shingle beach   A beach made of fine pebbles.

spit   A ridge of sand or pebbles joined to the land at one end and sticking out into the ocean at the other.

stack   A pillar of rock standing in the ocean near cliffs.

tides   The rise and fall of the level of the oceans and seas twice a day.

wave   A regular movement of the surface of water caused by the wind.

wave-cut platform   A level area of rock at the base of a sea cliff formed when waves erode the bottom of the cliff, making the top of the cliff collapse.

Index